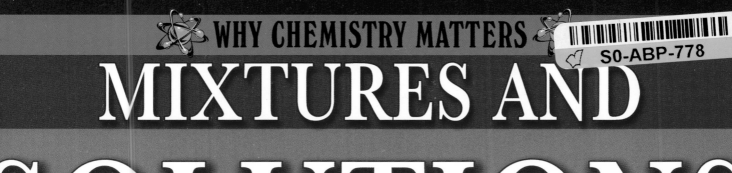

WHY CHEMISTRY MATTERS

SO-ABP-778

MIXTURES AND
SOLUTIONS

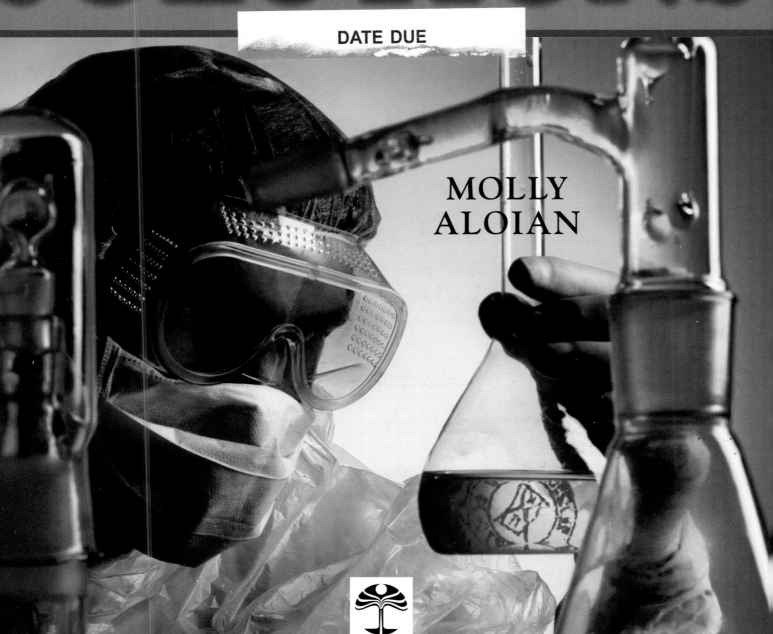

DATE DUE

MOLLY
ALOIAN

Crabtree Publishing Company
www.crabtreebooks.com

Crabtree Publishing Company

www.crabtreebooks.com

Author: Molly Aloian
Coordinating editor: Chester Fisher
Series editor: Scholastic Ventures
Project manager: Kavita Lad (Q2AMEDIA)
Art direction: Dibakar Acharjee (Q2AMEDIA)
Cover design: Ranjan Singh (Q2AMEDIA)
Design: Neha Sethi (Q2AMEDIA)
Photo research: Anju Pathak (Q2AMEDIA)
Editor: Adrianna Morganelli
Proofreader: Reagan Miller
Project coordinator: Robert Walker
Production coordinator: Katherine Kantor
Font management: Mike Golka
Prepress technicians: Samara Parent, Ken Wright

Photographs:
Cover: Kate Leigh/Istockphoto; Title page: Andrey Kiselev/Fotolia; P4: The London Art Archive/Alamy; P5: Lexx/Istockphoto (top); P5: Jan Kaliciak/Shutterstock (middle); P6: Michael D. Brown/Shutterstock; P7: Weldon Schloneger/Shutterstock (top), Jan Kaliciak/Shutterstock (middle); P8: Phil Degginger/Alamy; P9: Wildlife GmbH/Alamy (top), Jan Kaliciak/Shutterstock (middle); P10: Radu Razvan/Shutterstock; P11: Jan Kaliciak/Shutterstock (right); P12: Charles Outcalt/Dreamstime; P13: Bob Kupbens/Istockphoto (top); P13: Danabeth555/BigStockPhoto (bottom); P14: Jonaldm/BigStockPhoto; P15: Kenneth C. Zirkel/Istockphoto (top); P15: Muellek/Shutterstock (bottom); P16: Ruchos/Istockphoto; P17: Q2A Media (left), Jan Kaliciak/Shutterstock (right); P18: Mikko Pitkanen/Shutterstock; P19: Farawaykid/Shutterstock (top); P19: Luca Medical/Alamy (bottom); P20: Chris S/BigStockPhoto; P21: Artem Mazunov/Shutterstock; P22: Richard Levine/Alamy; P23: Q2A Media (top), Jan Kaliciak/Shutterstock (bottom); P24: Q2A Media; P25: Q2A Media; P26: Joshua Blake/Istockphoto; P27: Serthom/Shutterstock; P28: Can Balcioglu/Shutterstock; P29: Sciencephotos/Alamy (left), Jan Kaliciak/Shutterstock (right)

Library and Archives Canada Cataloguing in Publication

Aloian, Molly
    Mixtures and solutions / Molly Aloian.

(Why chemistry matters)
Includes index.
ISBN 978-0-7787-4243-2 (bound).--ISBN 978-0-7787-4250-0 (pbk.)

    1. Solution (Chemistry)--Juvenile literature. 2. Mixtures--Juvenile literature. 3. Matter--Properties--Juvenile literature. 4. Chemistry--Juvenile literature. I. Title. II. Series.

QD541.A46 2008   j541'.34   C2008-904140-2

Library of Congress Cataloging-in-Publication Data

Aloian, Molly.
    Mixtures and solutions / Molly Aloian.
       p. cm. -- (Why chemistry matters)
    Includes index.
    ISBN-13: 978-0-7787-4250-0 (pbk. : alk. paper)
    ISBN-10: 0-7787-4250-4 (pbk. : alk. paper)
    ISBN-13: 978-0-7787-4243-2 (reinforced library binding : alk. paper)
    ISBN-10: 0-7787-4243-1 (reinforced library binding : alk. paper)
    1. Solution (Chemistry)--Juvenile literature. 2. Mixtures--Juvenile literature. 3. Matter--Properties--Juvenile literature. 4. Chemistry--Juvenile literature. I. Title.
    QD541.A46 2009
    541'.34--dc22
                                    2008028896

Published in Canada
Crabtree Publishing
616 Welland Ave.
St. Catharines, ON
L2M 5V6

Published in the United States
Crabtree Publishing
PMB16A
350 Fifth Ave., Suite 3308
New York, NY 10118

Published in the United Kingdom
Crabtree Publishing
White Cross Mills
High Town, Lancaster
LA1 4XS

Published in Australia
Crabtree Publishing
386 Mt. Alexander Rd.
Ascot Vale (Melbourne)
VIC 3032

Contents

What is Matter?

Matter is everywhere. All living things and non-living things are matter. In fact, anything that occupies space and has **mass** is matter. Mass is related to weight, which is the pull of **gravity** on an object. Water and air are both composed of matter. Matter is sometimes a pure substance. A pure substance is the same substance throughout. Matter can also be a mixture or a **solution**.

The Greek philosopher Democritus created the name "atom."

Molecules are tiny **particles** of matter. Molecules are too small for anyone to see, even under a powerful microscope. There are billions of molecules in just one tiny grain of sand. Molecules contain even tinier particles called **atoms**. The atoms join together to form molecules. For example, in an oxygen molecule, there are two oxygen atoms joined together. There are only about 100 different kinds of atoms, but there are thousands of different molecules. Molecules contain different combinations of atoms. For example, a salt molecule is different from a sugar molecule because it contains a different combination of atoms.

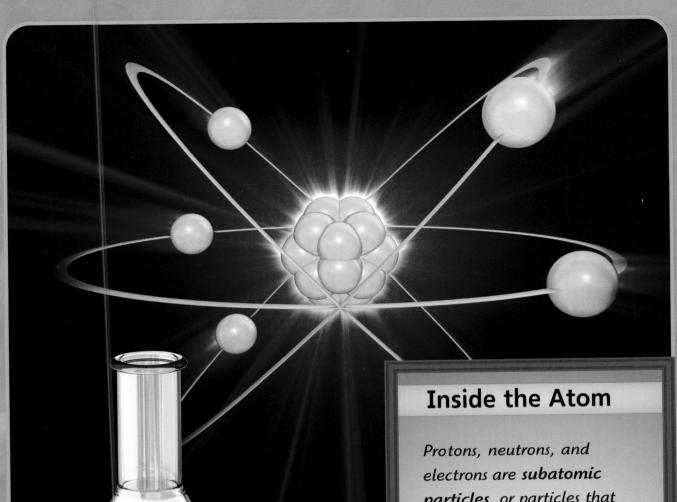

Most of the matter in an atom is in the core, called the nucleus.

Inside the Atom

*Protons, neutrons, and electrons are **subatomic particles**, or particles that are part of an atom. Protons and electrons have electrical charges. Protons have a positive charge. Electrons have a negative charge. Neutrons have no electrical charge; they are neutral. A positively charged proton attracts a negatively charged electron and **repels** another positive charge. A negatively charged electron attracts a positively charged proton and repels another negative charge.*

It is very hard to imagine the size of molecules and atoms. If each person on Earth was the size of one atom, all the people alive today would fit on the head of one pin. The amount of atoms in one glass of water is equal to all the grains of sand on all the beaches on Earth!

All About Elements

Molecules that contain one kind of atom are called **elements**. Elements are the purest type of matter. They are simple, natural substances. Each atom in an element has the same number of protons.

There are about 100 different elements. They can combine with each other to create every substance on Earth. There are about 90 elements that occur naturally on Earth, including the hydrogen found in water, the neon in street signs, and the iron in nails. Scientists created the other elements. They made a chart of all elements. It is the Periodic Table of the Elements. The table lists the elements in order of how many protons they have.

The position of an element in the table shows whether it is a metal, a nonmetal, or a metalloid. Over half of all elements are metals. Gold is a metal. There are 16 nonmetals. Gases, including helium, are nonmetals. There are seven metalloids. Metalloids are neither metals nor nonmetals, but they can have characteristics of metals or nonmetals. Silicon is a metalloid. Computer microchips contain silicon.

This is the Periodic Table of the Elements. Iron, copper, helium, hydrogen, and oxygen are all elements.

1 H Hydrogen 1.0079																	2 He Helium 4.0026
3 Li Lithium 6.941	4 Be Beryllium 9.0122											5 B Boron 10.881	6 C Carbon 12.0107	7 N Nitrogen 14.0067	8 O Oxygen 15.9994	9 F Fluorine 18.9984	10 Ne Neon 20.1797
11 Na Sodium 22.9897	12 Mg Magnesium 24.305											13 Al Aluminum 26.9815	14 Si Silicon 28.0855	15 P Phosphorus 30.9738	16 S Sulfur 32.065	17 Cl Chlorine 35.453	18 Ar Argon 39.948
19 K Potassium 39.098	20 Ca Calcium 40.078	21 Sc Scandium 44.9559	22 Ti Titanium 47.867	23 V Vanadium 50.9415	24 Cr Chromium 51.9961	25 Mn Manganese 54.938	26 Fe Iron 55.845	27 Co Cobalt 58.9332	28 Ni Nickel 58.6934	29 Cu Copper 63.546	30 Zn Zinc 65.409	31 Ga Gallium 69.723	32 Ge Germanium 72.64	33 As Arsenic 74.9216	34 Se Selenium 78.96	35 Br Bromine 79.904	36 Kr Krypton 83.798
37 Rb Rubidium 85.4678	38 Sr Strontium 87.62	39 Y Yttrium 88.9059	40 Zr Zirconium 91.224	41 Nb Niobium 92.9064	42 Mo Molybdenum 95.94	43 Tc Technetium (98)	44 Ru Ruthenium 101.07	45 Rh Rhodium 102.9055	46 Pd Palladium 106.42	47 Ag Silver 107.8682	48 Cd Cadmium 112.411	49 In Indium 114.818	50 Sn Tin 118.71	51 Sb Antimony 121.76	52 Te Tellurium 127.6	53 I Iodine 126.9045	54 Xe Xenon 131.293
55 Cs Cesium 132.9055	56 Ba Barium 137.327		72 Hf Hafnium 178.49	73 Ta Tantalum 180.9479	74 W Tungsten 183.84	75 Re Rhenium 186.207	76 Os Osmium 190.23	77 Ir Iridium 192.217	78 Pt Platinum 195.078	79 Au Gold 196.9665	80 Hg Mercury 200.59	81 Tl Thallium 204.3833	82 Pb Lead 207.2	83 Bi Bismuth 208.9804	84 Po Polonium (209)	85 At Astatine (210)	86 Rn Radon (222)
87 Fr Francium (223)	88 Ra Radium (226)		104 Rf Rutherfordium (261)	105 Db Dubnium (262)	106 Sg Seaborgium (266)	107 Bh Bohrium (264)	108 Hs Hassium (277)	109 Mt Meitnerium (268)	110 Ds Darmstadtium (271)	111 Rg Roentgenium (272)	112 Uub Ununbium (277)						

57 La Lanthanum 138.9055	58 Ce Cerium 140.116	59 Pr Praseodymium 140.9077	60 Nd Neodymium 144.24	61 Pm Promethium (145)	62 Sm Samarium 150.36	63 Eu Europium 151.964	64 Gd Gadolinium 157.25	65 Tb Terbium 158.9253	66 Dy Dysprosium 162.5	67 Ho Holmium 164.9303	68 Er Erbium 167.259	69 Tm Thulium 168.9342	70 Yb Ytterbium 173.04	71 Lu Lutetium 174.967
89 Ac Actinium 227.03	90 Th Thorium 232.0381	91 Pa Protactinium 231.0359	92 U Uranium 238.0289	93 Np Neptunium (237)	94 Pu Plutonium (244)	95 Am Americium (243)	96 Cm Curium (247)	97 Bk Berkelium (247)	98 Cf Californium (251)	99 Es Einsteinium (252)	100 Fm Fermium (257)	101 Md Mendelevium (258)	102 No Nobelium (259)	103 Lr Lawrencium (262)

This iceberg is a solid. Like all solids, it keeps the same shape.

States of Matter

Solids, gases, and liquids are states of matter. When a substance changes from one state of matter to another, the temperature of its molecules must increase or decrease. For example, water molecules get warmer and gain energy if they are heated on a stove. They also move faster. Water molecules get cooler and lose energy if they are cooled in a freezer. They move slowly.

Every element has a **chemical symbol**. People use these chemical symbols to write the names of elements. The symbols have either one or two letters. The first letter is always a capital letter. The second letter is always lower case. For example, the symbol for gold is Au. The symbol for carbon is C.

Properties

People identify a material by looking at its **physical properties**. Color, taste, smell, and state of matter are examples of physical properties. A change in a material's physical properties is a physical change. Physical changes include a change in size or shape. For example, when water freezes, it changes from a liquid to a solid. It is still water, but the temperature of its molecules has decreased and its state of matter is different.

People can also identify substances by how they react with other substances. This reaction is a **chemical property**. A change in a material's chemical properties is a chemical change. Chemical changes include bubbles of gas in liquids. For example, when a person mixes baking soda and vinegar together, the chemical change creates bubbles of carbon dioxide gas.

When two or more different kinds of atoms **bond**, or join, the new substance is a **compound**. The formation of a compound is a chemical change. This means that one substance changes into another. Compounds are combinations of elements. Sugar, salt, water, and nylon are compounds.

Mixing vinegar and baking soda together produces water and sodium acetate.

Iron sulfide is a compound. It contains iron and sulfur.

Burning Wood

*When wood burns in a fireplace, it changes into new materials. The wood burns and joins with oxygen in the air. Water vapor, carbon dioxide, and a soft gray material called **ash** form as a result. Water vapor is water in a gas state. Both water vapor and carbon dioxide are gases. They are colorless and odorless. They are new materials that have different properties than the wood.*

In a **mixture**, the atoms do not make a new, different substance. They do not combine chemically. The formation of a mixture is a physical change. Most of the matter on Earth is a mixture. Many man-made substances, such as nylon, paint, and concrete, are also mixtures.

Ions

Atoms usually have the same number of protons as electrons, so their electrical charges cancel each other out. So most atoms are neutral and have no overall electrical charge. Some atoms can gain or lose electrons, however. These electrically charged atoms are **ions**. If an atom gains electrons, it contains more negatively charged particles than positively charged particles. As a result, the atom has a negative charge. Negatively charged ions are **anions**. An atom becomes positively charged if it loses electrons. Positively charged ions are **cations**.

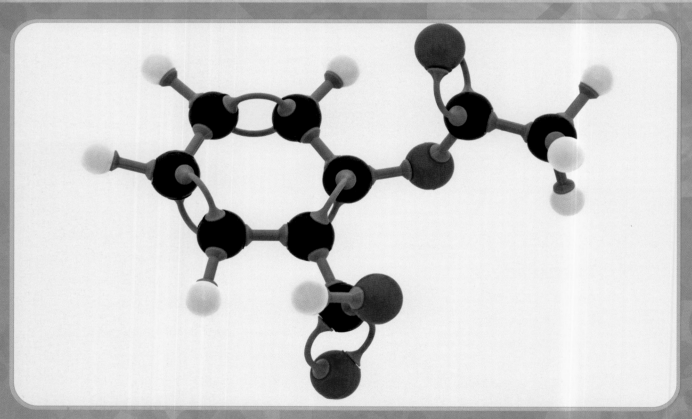

This model of a molecule is a ball-and-spoke model.

When a metal atom loses an electron to a nonmetal atom, an **ionic compound** forms. The metal atom becomes a cation and the nonmetal atom becomes an anion. The attraction of their opposite charges holds the two together. As a result, they form an ionic compound.

Sodium chloride, or table salt, is an example of an ionic compound. A sodium atom contains 11 protons and 11 electrons. It is neutral. A chlorine atom is also neutral because it contains 17 protons and 17 electrons. Neutral sodium atoms react with neutral chlorine atoms and each sodium atom loses an electron. The chlorine atoms gain the electrons. This creates sodium cations and chlorine anions. Their opposite electrical charges attract them to each other, creating sodium chloride.

Covalent compounds have atoms of different elements that share electrons. Metals usually share electrons with nonmetals. Sharing electrons bonds the atoms together to form new molecules. Water is an example of a **covalent compound**.

Make a Model

To make a water model, you need an atom of oxygen and two atoms of hydrogen. Use red clay to make the oxygen atom. Make the oxygen atom bigger than the hydrogen atoms. Use blue clay to form the hydrogen atoms. Stick the toothpicks into the red oxygen atom and then stick the blue hydrogen atoms on the ends. The toothpicks are the bonds.

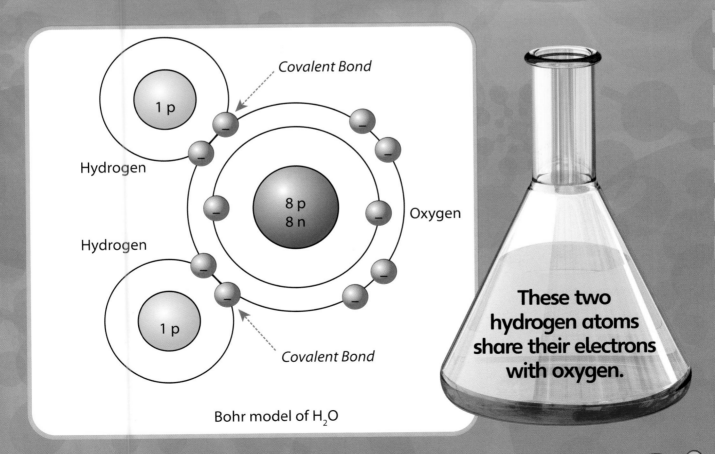

Covalent Bond

1 p

Hydrogen

8 p
8 n

Oxygen

Hydrogen

1 p

Covalent Bond

Bohr model of H_2O

These two hydrogen atoms share their electrons with oxygen.

Compounds

Two or more types of atoms joined together form a compound. Compounds contain elements in fixed proportions, which means the amounts of each ingredient cannot vary. Chalk is an example of a compound. One molecule of chalk contains one atom of calcium, one atom of carbon, and three atoms of oxygen.

A compound contains two or more ingredients, but it is a completely different substance from its ingredients. A molecule is the smallest possible quantity of any compound. For example, there are two hydrogen atoms and one oxygen atom in a water molecule. The chemical formula for water is H_2O. There are billions of water molecules, billions of hydrogen atoms, and billions of oxygen atoms in just one drop of water. Scientists call water H_2O no matter how many molecules are in a specific quantity of water. Two hydrogen atoms and one oxygen atom is the smallest amount of water it is possible to have in one place. The proportions of hydrogen and oxygen are fixed.

Rocks are usually mixtures of compounds.

The atoms in a compound bond tightly together. To break compounds apart, there must be a chemical reaction. People use energy to create a chemical reaction. Heat, light, and electricity are forms of energy. In 1799, British chemist Humphry Davy passed an electrical current through some compounds. This process is **electrolysis**. Davy discovered that he could separate compounds into their component elements.

A piece of chalk is brittle, which means it will break easily. This is a physical property.

Pass the Sugar

Sugar is a solid. It is a compound of hydrogen, oxygen, and carbon. Heating sugar to a high temperature causes a chemical reaction. Heat causes the sugar to break apart into its component elements. It causes hydrogen and oxygen to join and form water vapor. The water vapor enters the air. Carbon, a black solid, is all that remains.

Sugar, or sucrose, occurs naturally in most plants.

13

Mixtures

Most things on Earth are mixtures. Mixtures are composed of several **pure substances**. In a mixture, the substances put together do not make a new, different substance. They do not combine chemically. The substances keep their own properties. Unlike a compound, the substances in a mixture can be physically separated. Mixtures can contain elements, compounds, or both.

Air is a mixture of gases. It contains nitrogen, oxygen, argon, and carbon dioxide. There are also water and dust particles in air. Air contains 78 percent nitrogen, 21 percent oxygen, 0.93 percent argon, and 0.03 percent carbon dioxide. The water molecules separate from the rest of air very easily. The molecules separate as rain or dew.

This dew has separated from the water in the air.

Toothpaste

Toothpaste is a soft solid. It is a mixture of liquids and small sandy particles called abrasives. The abrasives help remove plaque from your teeth and keep your teeth white. Plaque is bacteria. The ingredients in toothpastes are evenly distributed. But the different ingredients can vary, which gives toothpastes their different colors and flavors.

Toothpaste contains compounds called fluorides.

You can make a mixture in many ways. For example, there can be any amount of salt and pepper in a mixture of salt and pepper. In the same way, there can be any amount of apples, oranges, and bananas in a fruit salad. A fruit salad is an example of a mixture. The ingredients in a fruit salad do not join together and can be easily separated from one another.

A salad dressing, such as vinaigrette, is a mixture. It contains oil and vinegar. Vinegar contains acetic acid and water. If you shake a bottle of vinaigrette, the oil and water mix, but they do not dissolve in each other. If you let the bottle sit for a few minutes, the oil remains on the top and the vinegar remains on the bottom.

The sauce, cheese, and other toppings on this pizza are not joined together. You could separate them easily.

Same or Different?

Ocean water is a mixture. It contains water and many dissolved solids such as chloride, sodium, sulfate, magnesium, and calcium. You cannot see the dissolved solids, however. This is because ocean water is a **homogeneous mixture**. A homogeneous mixture has the same uniform appearance and composition throughout. Dissolving a small amount of sugar in some water creates a homogeneous mixture. You cannot see the dissolved sugar. The prefix "homo" is a sign of sameness. Many homogeneous mixtures are solutions.

This sidewalk is concrete. If you look closely, you can see the sand and rocks in the cement mixture.

A **heterogeneous mixture** has larger parts that you can see. It consists of visibly different substances or states of matter. A pile of rocks is a heterogeneous mixture. The rocks are mixtures of minerals. Concrete is another heterogeneous mixture. It is a mixture of cement, water, sand, and other particles of rocks. The cement becomes hard, but the cement and other ingredients do not combine chemically. The ingredients keep their own properties. The prefix "hetero" is a sign of difference.

The particles of flour in this suspension have settled. Large particles settle more quickly than do small particles.

Two in One

Combining iron and sulfur powder creates a mixture. It is a mixture of two elements. Stirring the powder with a magnet or swirling the powder with a magnet under the container separates the components of the mixture. The iron will stick to the magnet. Heating the mixture creates a compound called iron sulfide. The iron sulfide will start to glow.

A **suspension** is a mixture that contains a liquid in which particles settle to the bottom over time. The particles in a suspension separate when they stand, or rest, for a period of time. For example, a mixture of flour and water is a suspension. The flour separates from the water when the mixture stands for a period of time. A suspension is often a cloudy mixture.

Alloys

An **alloy** is a mixture. It consists of a metal and one or more other elements. An alloy usually has different properties than the properties of its component elements. Aluminum, bronze, brass, and steel are examples of alloys. People use alloys of gold and copper to make jewelry. The copper helps make the gold strong. People make certain alloys by melting and mixing two or more metals. For example, people make the alloy brass by mixing copper and zinc. Bronze, which people use for statues and medals, is an alloy of tin and copper.

Some people classify alloys by the number of their components. An alloy with two components is a binary alloy. Brass and bronze are binary alloys. An alloy with three components is a ternary alloy. Stellite is a ternary alloy that companies use to make saw blades and other parts for machinery.

Amalgam is an alloy that contains mercury and other elements. Amalgam is a liquid first, but it quickly becomes hard. Some dentists use amalgam to fill cavities in people's teeth.

Copper is a component of various alloys.

Steel is an alloy of iron and other elements. Some alloys contain small amounts of nonmetallic elements, such as carbon. Adding just a tiny amount of carbon to steel makes steel stronger. People use carbon-steel alloys in weapons, but carbon-steel tends to rust when exposed to air and moisture. There are many types of steel.

People make alloy wheels from an alloy of aluminum or magnesium.

Stainless Steel

*There are different types of stainless steel. Stainless steel is strong and does not stain, **corrode**, or rust as easily as ordinary steel. To corrode means to wear away. Stainless steel contains nickel and chromium. Cookware, cutlery, hardware, major appliances including refrigerators and stoves, surgical instruments, and other items contain stainless steel. Doctors use stainless steel instruments when they are performing surgeries. Stainless steel is 100 percent recyclable.*

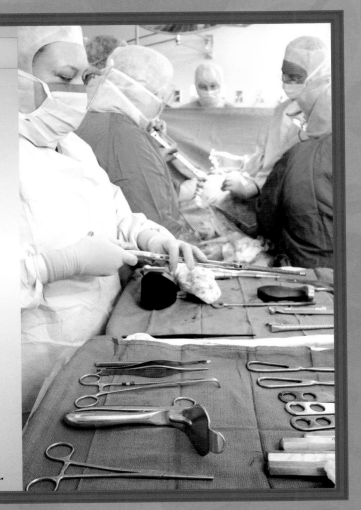

These medical tools are made from stainless steel.

Colloids

A **colloid** is also a mixture. In a colloid, one substance is dispersed throughout another. The particles in a colloid are minute, or extremely tiny. They are colloidal particles. The colloidal particles remain mixed because they constantly knock into one another. Some colloids, such as mayonnaise and aerosol sprays, are man-made. Others, including fog and clouds, occur naturally.

A colloid is sometimes called a colloidal system. Colloidal systems are combinations of solids, liquids, and gases. Fog and clouds are colloids of a liquid in a gas. They are water droplets, which are liquid, in air, which is a gas. The substance found in the greater amount in the colloid is called the dispersing medium. The substance found in the lesser amount is called the dispersed phase. Gel, such as jelly, is a colloid of a solid in a liquid. It is a colloid because a solid (fruit) is the dispersing medium and a liquid (the jelly) is the dispersed phase.

The fog in this valley is a colloid.

People see the Tyndall effect from the dust in air when sunlight shines in a window.

If a person shines a beam of light through a colloid, the light will scatter on the particles of the colloid. For example, when a person shines their car headlights through fog, the light will scatter and reveal the particles within the fog. This is sometimes called the Tyndall effect, because a physicist named John Tyndall discovered it.

Large Molecules

Colloids are large molecules, such as proteins, or groups of molecules. Proteins are substances that consist of chains of amino acids. They contain the elements carbon, hydrogen, nitrogen, oxygen, and often sulfur. Large molecules or groups of molecules are common in colloids because they remain suspended indefinitely.

Solutions

A solution is a type of mixture. It is a homogeneous mixture composed of two or more substances. The molecules in a solution are too small to see. For example, you cannot see sugar mixed in water. The sugar dissolves and seems to disappear, and the sugar molecules distribute evenly throughout the water. Many people drink powdered drinks. These drinks are a solution. They blend water, sugar, and solid crystals or powder, which add flavor.

Blood is both a solution and a suspension. Blood is a solution because it contains gases and dissolved solids, such as sugars. Blood is a suspension because there are solids suspended in the blood. Red blood cells, white blood cells, and large proteins are some of the solids suspended in the blood. Doctors take blood samples and perform blood tests on the tubes of blood. Before the doctors perform their tests, a special machine spins the test tubes of blood at very high speeds. The machine pulls the suspended particles to the bottom of the tube.

Drinks made from powdered mixes are not pure substances. They are solutions.

Dissolving table salt in water makes a saline, or salty, water solution.

Solutes and Solvents

There are solutes and solvents in a mixture. The solute dissolves in another substance. The solvent is the substance that dissolves the solute. For example, in a solution of water and sugar, the sugar is the solute and the water is the solvent. When no more of a solute can dissolve into a solvent, the solution is saturated.

Solubility is the ability of the **solvent** to dissolve the **solute**. Temperature affects a solvent's solubility. Hot solvents dissolve solutes faster than do solvents that are room temperature or colder.

Getting the Solution

Some solutions are weak. A weak solution contains a small amount of material dissolved in it. It is a **dilute** solution. Other solutions are strong. A strong solution contains a large amount of material dissolved in it. It is a **concentrated** solution. As the amount of the material increases, the solution becomes more concentrated.

Solutions can also be saturated, unsaturated, or supersaturated. A saturated solution is a solution in which the maximum amount of solvent dissolved at a particular temperature. Additional solute will sit as crystals on the bottom of the solution.

This is a strong powdered drink solution. It is darker than the weak powdered drink.

This student is making an unsaturated solution.

For example, scientists believe that the solubility of table salt in water is 1.3 ounces (37 grams) per 3.5 ounces (103 milliliters) of water. A solution containing 1.3 ounces (37 grams) of table salt in 3.5 ounces (103 milliliters) of water is a saturated solution; it cannot hold any more table salt. An unsaturated solution is a solution in which more solute can be dissolved into the solvent at a particular temperature. For example, a solution with 0.18 ounces (5 grams) of table salt in 3.5 ounces (103 milliliters) of water is unsaturated.

In a saturated solution, a slight drop in temperature will usually cause some of the solute to **crystallize** out of the solution. If this does not happen, the phenomenon is supercooling, and the solution is supersaturated.

Make a Solution

It is very easy to make a solution. All you need is a solvent, a solute, and a system. A system is a container. Use water for the solvent and sugar for the solute. Place the solute into the solvent. The concentration of the substances will be equal throughout the system. The concentration of sugar in the water will be the same at the bottom, middle, and top of the container.

More Solutions

A solid dissolved in a liquid is usually a solution. Solids dissolved in liquids can dissolve at different speeds. The speed at which the solid dissolves depends on the size of the solid. Small particles dissolve faster than large particles. Stirring the solution also makes a solid dissolve faster.

A gas dissolved in a liquid is also a solution. Oxygen dissolves in lakes, rivers, and oceans. Fish and other animals need the oxygen to survive. They breathe the oxygen dissolved in the water.

A liquid dissolved in a different liquid is a solution. Some liquids, including ethylene glycol, dissolve in water. **Antifreeze** is a solution of water and ethylene glycol. People put antifreeze in their car radiators to prevent water in the radiator from freezing. Antifreeze freezes at a lower temperature than water.

A can of soda is a solution of water and carbon dioxide. The solution is mixed under pressure.

This fish is breathing the solution of oxygen dissolved in water.

Oil is a liquid that does not dissolve in water. This is the reason people should never use water to try to extinguish burning oil. When people throw water on burning oil, the fire spreads.

A metal alloy is an example of a solution of two solids. Most American coins are made from an alloy of copper and nickel. The alloy is silver-colored. It is very hard and durable. Dimes and quarters have an inner layer of pure copper, which can be seen by looking at the edges of a coin. Steel is another important solid solution.

Two Gases

In a solution of two gases, it is often difficult to determine which gas is dissolved (the solute) and which gas is the dissolver (the solvent). In a solution of two gases, the component present in the solution in the largest amount is the solvent. The component present in the smaller amount is the solute.

Separating Solutions

In a solution, one material only seems to disappear into another. But the parts of a solution can be separated from one another. If a solid dissolved in a liquid is left in the air, it will separate. The liquid **evaporates**, leaving the solid behind.

This kettle contains water. Water molecules escape as steam, which is a gas.

When a substances changes from one state of matter to another, the temperature of its molecules must increase or decrease. Remember that changes in state of matter are physical changes, not chemical changes. Heating a solution of a gas and a liquid causes the gas to escape into the air. The liquid remains.

It is also simple to separate solutions of liquids. Heating the solution slowly causes each liquid to change into a gas. Each liquid changes to a gas at a different temperature. As each liquid disperses, the gas remains. Scientists use this process to separate the different parts of air. Cooling air eventually turns the air into a liquid. Warming up the air very slowly will cause the nitrogen in air to boil. Nitrogen boils at a lower temperature than does oxygen. Nitrogen becomes a gas before oxygen does. This leaves the oxygen behind. So scientists can collect the two gases separately.

Chromatography

Chromatography is a way of separating and identifying mixtures, especially colored ones. Surprisingly, black ink contains a mixture of colors, and it is possible to separate the colors from one another. Molecules of ink have different characteristics, including size and solubility. When a line of black ink on a piece of filter paper touches a solution of rubbing alcohol, the alcohol moves up the paper, separating the colors in the ink.

The bottom of this paper was barely touching the liquid. The liquid moved up the paper and separated the colors in the ink.

Glossary

abrasive A substance used for grinding, smoothing, or polishing

alloy A mixture of a metal and one or more elements

amalgam An alloy of mercury

anion A negatively charged ion

antifreeze A substance added to liquid to stop it from freezing

ash The solid that remains after a material is burned

atom Tiny particle

bond The means by which atoms, ions, or groups of atoms are held together

cation A positively charged ion

chemical property A characteristic that shows how something will react

chemical symbol A short way of writing the name of an element

chromatography A way of separating and identifying mixtures, especially colored ones

colloid A mixture with particles that are between that of solutions and suspensions

compound Substances that are made of two or more different types of atoms

concentrated Describing something that contains a large amount of material

corrode To be eaten or worn away gradually

covalent compound A compound that is formed when atoms join and share electrons

crystallize To cause to form crystals

dilute Describing something that contains a small amount of material

electrolysis Producing chemical changes by passing an electric current through a conductor

element A material made from one kind of atom

evaporate To turn into vapor

gravity A force of attraction between particles that happens because of their mass

heterogeneous mixture A mixture wherein the parts are dissimilar

homogeneous mixture A mixture wherein the parts are similar

ion An atom or a group of atoms with an electric charge

ionic compound An atom that has lost an electron

mass A quantity of matter that holds together

matter Anything that occupies space and has mass

mixture substance made of elements or compounds that are not joined chemically

molecule two or more atoms held together by chemical bonds

nucleus The center of an atom

particle A very small part of matter

physical property A characteristic that can be seen or measured without changing what a material is made of

plaque A sticky, colorless film on teeth that is made of bacteria

pure substance Matter that is the same throughout

repel To keep away

solubility The amount of a substance that will dissolve in another substance

solute A dissolving substance

solution A mixture in which one substance dissolves in another

solvent A substance that dissolves a solute

state of matter Whether something is a solid, a liquid, or a gas

subatomic particle The particles inside an atom

suspension A mixture that contains a liquid in which particles settle to the bottom over time

Index

Web Finder

http://www.chem4kids.com/files/matter_mixture.html
http://www.chem4kids.com/files/matter_solution.html
http://www.scienceclarified.com/index.html
http://www.fossweb.com/modules3-6/index.html
http://www.udel.edu/sine/students/mixtures/index.html
http://www.elmhurst.edu/~chm/vchembook/106Amixture.html

Printed in the U.S.A.